piano allsorts
collection

Edited and compiled by
CAROL BARRATT

Chester Music
(A division of Music Sales Limited)
8/9 Frith Street London W1V 5TZ

preface

This repertoire book contains pieces ranging from the 17th to the
20th centuries, and can be used as a supplementary book to
THE NEXT STEP PIANO COURSE book 2 and upwards.

Carol Barratt

Cover design by Chloë Alexander.
Printed in Great Britain by Printwise (Haverhill) Limited, Haverhill, Suffolk.

contents

QUICK MARCH

CAROL BARRATT

(R.H. stays in this position
and L.H. crosses over)

CHEVY CHASE

This tune dates from c.1600.
English Folk Song

ARRANGED BY CAROL BARRATT

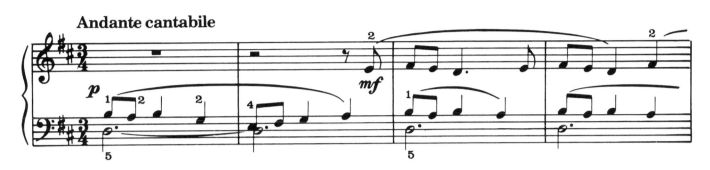

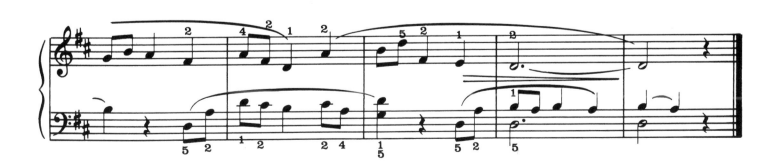

BUTTON-DOWN BLUES

CAROL BARRATT

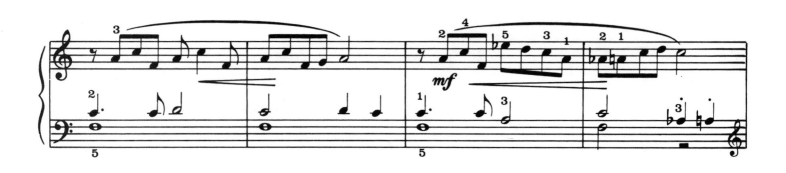

MINUET

W.A. MOZART (1756-1791)

THE SYCAMORE

A Concert Rag

S. JOPLIN (1868-1917)
Simplified by Carol Barratt

Slow march time

LITTLE PRELUDE

C. FRANCK (1822-1890)
Simplified by Carol Barratt

Adagio semplice

BADINAGE

A. CORELLI (1653-1713)

Moderato

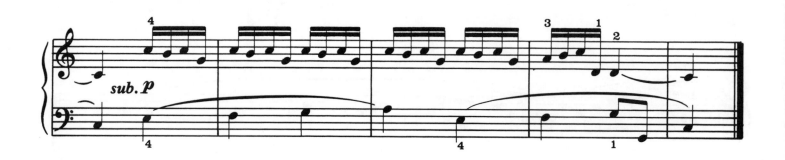

HOBNOBS

CAROL BARRATT

MORNING SONG

Try writing out this piece in your manuscript book, using flats
instead of sharps (e.g. the first note in the treble clef will be B♭).
The key signature has been omitted to make this easier.

French Folk Song

ARRANGED BY CAROL BARRATT

SHEEP SHEARING

Swedish Folk Song

ARRANGED BY CAROL BARRATT

MINUET I

J.S. BACH (1685-1750)

Moderato

MINUET II

This is the same as Minuet I, except that the right hand tune is now
in the left hand, and the left hand tune is now in the right hand!

J.S. BACH (1685-1750)

15

ÉCOSSAISE

F. SCHUBERT (1797-1828)

TINK-A-TINK

This piece is an arrangement of a 17th century fiddle tune,
and is taken from a collection of traditional English and
Scottish dance tunes called 'Playford's Dancing Master'.

TRADITIONAL (17TH CENTURY)
ARRANGED BY CAROL BARRATT

VARIATIONS ON A RUSSIAN FOLK TUNE

CAROL BARRATT

Theme

18

ALBUM LEAF

E. GRIEG (1843-1907)
Simplified by Carol Barratt

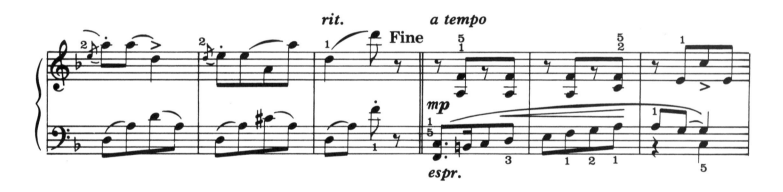

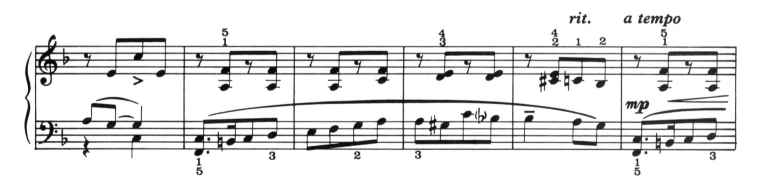

19

PIANO MUSIC FOR YOUNG AND OLD

An excerpt from No.24

C. NIELSEN (1865-1931)

THE MAN WITH THE BAGPIPES

French Folk Tune

ARRANGED BY CAROL BARRATT

21

SONATINA IN G

First Movement

A. DIABELLI (1781-1858)

Allegro moderato

MAZURKA

An excerpt from Op.67 No.2

F. CHOPIN (1810-1849)
Simplified by Carol Barratt

24

A RUMBA FOR ROBIN

CAROL BARRATT

TARANTELLA

CAROL BARRATT

REQUIEM FOR A LITTLE BIRD

G. SANDRÉ (1843-1916)

SANDY'S SHUFFLE

CAROL BARRATT

ENGLISH DANCE

K. VON DITTERSDORF (1739-1799)

GAVOTTE

G.F. HANDEL (1685-1759)

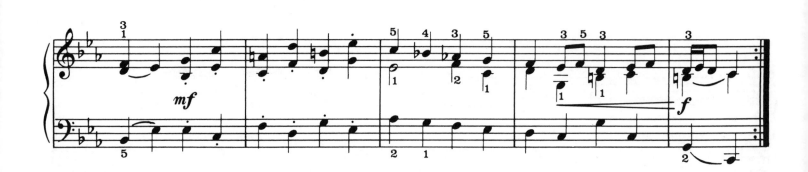

30

QUICK MARCH

D. KABALEVSKY (1904-1987)

HAPPY STORY

D. KABALEVSKY (1904-1987)

31

NEEDLES AND PINS

Another title for this piece is 'I'm Ninety-five'.
English Morris Dance

ARRANGED BY CAROL BARRATT

MINUET IN D

W.A. MOZART (1756-1791)

Allegro moderato

THREE PLUS FOUR

CAROL BARRATT

34

VERSETTO

If you can't stretch the octave, play the lower note in each case.

D. ZIPOLI (1688-1726)

35

THE DUCK
from Peter And The Wolf

S. PROKOFIEV (1891-1953)
Simplified by Carol Barratt

SHOO, FLY

American Folk Song

ARRANGED BY CAROL BARRATT

FOUR LITTLE WEAVERS

Dutch Folk Song

ARRANGED BY CAROL BARRATT

TWO GERMAN DANCES

F.J. HAYDN (1732-1809)

TRIO
Con eleganza

German Dance No. 1. D.C.

39

MIDSUMMER FIRE
Swedish Folk Song

ARRANGED BY CAROL BARRATT

WHEN I HEAR THE BAGPIPES
Czech Folk Song

ARRANGED BY CAROL BARRATT

AN OLD DANCE

Moderato

D. KABALEVSKY (1904-1987)

ÉCOSSAISE

F. SCHUBERT (1797-1828)
Simplified by Carol Barratt

THE CHRYSANTHEMUM

An Afro-American Intermezzo

S. JOPLIN (1868-1917)
Simplified by Carol Barratt

SCHERZINO

CAROL BARRATT

Allegro con moto ♩ = 96–104

44

INTERMEZZO

M. GLINKA (1804-1857)

HAPPY AND SAD

This is the English translation of the original German title 'Lustig und traurig'.

L. VAN BEETHOVEN (1770-1827)

TANGO FOR REX

CAROL BARRATT

11/04 (52936)